Compiled by Rewa Mirpuri

PUBLISHED BY THE
ROTARY CLUB OF SINGAPORE
TEL: (65) 6737 2504, FAX: (65) 6442 1874
EMAIL: rtyinfo@rotary.org.sg **OR**
rewamirpuri@gmail.com
www.rotary.org.sg/bookofhumour.html
&
www.booksofhumour.com

ISBN No. 978-981-08-6467-5

@ Copyright Rewa Mirpuri, 2011

All rights reserved. No part of this publication may be produced, stored in a retrieval system, or transmitted in any form or by any means, electronic, mechanical, photocopying, recording, or otherwise, without the prior permission of the compiler.

Published by Rotary Club of Singapore
Tel: (65) 6737 2504 / 6241 9157.
Fax: (65) 6442 1874.
Email: rewamirpuri@gmail.com

Printed in Singapore

First Published in – June 11

First Reprint - July 2011

Second Reprint - January 2012

Third Reprint - April 2013

ENCORE!

The **BANK OF HUMOUR** was born out of the success of the first two editions, **BOOK OF HUMOUR** AND **BEST OF HUMOUR**, which have sold over 100,000 and 25,000 copies respectively. Be sure to add both these books to your collection to double your laughter, spice up your speech, liven up a party and delight your dinner guests.

ROTARY CLUB OF SINGAPORE
District 3310

MESSAGE
From former President, Republic of Singapore

I am impressed by the collection of jokes that Mr Mirpuri has gathered and has shared with his readers over the last 20 years. His first book published in June 1992 and his second in 2002 followed by the latest means that he has faithfully gathered jokes over the years, shared them with audiences in various social gatherings and published them in the three volumes.

I had a chance to briefly browse through his latest "Bank of Humour". I must say that the jokes I came across were downright hilarious, although some critics may find some even mischievous.

His latest compilation, 10 years after the last book, reflects his labour of love which he shares with his readers. I hope it will not only bring laughter to them but also allow them through supporting the book also raise funds for various charities, as it has done in the past.

I sincerely hope that "Bank of Humour" will be therapeutic to its readers and help them relax from the pressures and stress and strains of city life.

With best wishes,
Yours sincerely

S R NATHAN

ROTARY CLUB OF SINGAPORE
District 3310

MESSAGE

The "Book of Humour" series is indeed the most significant project of the Rotary Club of Singapore's World Community Service. It continues to prove as an outstanding success helping the Club to raise considerable funds to help the less fortunate and the needy in disaster stricken countries, far and near.

It is most enlightening that we are into the fourth print of this 3rd edition in the 'BOH' series, the **Bank of Humour**, following the tremendous popularity of the first two editions, **"Book of Humour"** and **"Best of Humour"**.

The pillar behind this ever successful project is none other than Rtn Rewa Mirpuri whose boundless sense of humour is exceptional. I would like to extend my gratitude to him and the BOH team who have made this an iconic project of the Club. I am confident that this will continue to be a sell-out and wish the **"Bank of Humour"** even greater success than ever before as it spreads cheers, laughter and peace through its jokes.

This is indeed **"Peace through Service and Above Self"**

Jimmy Ooi
78th President
Rotary Club of Singapore

PREFACE

This latest and 3rd edition BANK OF HUMOUR is dedicated to you.

Words are not enough to express my deep gratitude to all of you for your wonderful support to my first two editions, **Book of Humour** and **Best of Humour** which have become great runaway successes.

The phenomenal success of these two evergreen editions has inspired me to bring to you my 3rd new edition **BANK OF HUMOUR** where I have put in my new latest, witty and hilarious collection of jokes and anecdotes, well selected and tested, for your enjoyment.

This Book is guaranteed to make you laugh or full money refunded.

The appropriate title, **BANK OF HUMOUR**, has the same acronym BOH as the first two editions, befitting the **BOH Trust** initiated by **Rotary Club of Singapore** to collect and distribute the proceeds of these 3 Books to the poor and the needy under the World Community Service Programme.

In today's world, everyone appreciates a reason to laugh!
I wish you a very happy reading and lots of laughter.

Yours in humour,

Rewa Mirpuri

ACKNOWLEDGEMENT

This book is dedicated to all those who helped towards its creation.

The book would not have been possible without the kind help, support and contributions from all friends, well wishers, members of the Rotary Club of Singapore and the family of the compiler.

Knowing that this book is being produced for a good cause, everyone generously gave a helping hand.

It would be difficult to pinpoint all names as so many have helped in one way or another - like in evaluation and contribution of jokes, editing, cover design ideas, etc.

However it would not be right if some names, whose **outstanding** help, support and contribution, are missed from this acknowledgment.

They are **Past President Murli Chanrai,** for sponsoring the initial print and this third Reprint, **Past President Raymon Huang,** Rotarian **Robert Craiu** and **George Rewa** for their tireless efforts in proof reading, suggestions and scrutiny of the contents.

To all of you, a big "THANK YOU" for helping a good cause.

FRANCHISE

Many Rotary Clubs in various countries are enjoying the franchise of our humour books for their own Fund - Raising projects. Please email to our Club for more details.

CONTENTS

Starter's Delight	1
Marriage & Newlyweds	4
Wedding Anniversaries	12
Husbands & Wives	14
Men and Women	26
Mothers – in – law	38
Age matters	44
Family Life – Parents & Kids	56
Doctors and Patients	69
Lawyers & Judges	82
At the Pearly Gates, Churches	90
Business & Banks	102
Restaurants	107
Golf & other recreations	108
Signs & Definitions	114
At the bar	124
Country bumpkins	127
All the nations	137
Other Vocations	140
Computer related	144
Miscellaneous	148

Please consume this book in the light-hearted spirit it was compiled, and not as *"FACTS OF LIFE"*.

These jokes were compiled to evoke laughter – **for a good cause. Thank you!**

"Most fund raising projects for charities involve walking in the noon day sun behind a little white ball or eating heavy dinners which we then have to work off walking in the noon day sun behind a little white ball. Mr. Rewa has struck upon a more original and painless way of making people chuckle or laugh out loud while their wallets are being lightened. This is his third collection which shows how much this method is a success."

S Dhanabalan
Chairman, Temasek Holdings Pte Ltd.

"You don't stop laughing because you grow old.
You grow old because you stop laughing!"

Michael Pritchard

Starter's Delight

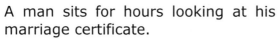

A man sits for hours looking at his marriage certificate.

Wife asks, "What are you looking for?"

The husband replies, **"I am looking for the expiry date."**

❖

Man: I want a divorce. My wife hasn't spoken to me in six months.

Lawyer: Better think it over. Wives like that are **hard to get!**

❖

Son: Mummy, when I was on the bus with Dad this morning he told me to give up my seat to a lady.

Mum: Well, you have done the right thing.

Son: But Mummy, I was sitting on **Daddy's lap**.

❖

One day, a man came home and was greeted by his wife dressed in a very sexy negligee.

"Tie me up, honey," she whispered to him, "and you can do **anything** you want."

So he tied her up and went golfing.

Patient: Doctor, the pills you gave me have made me constipated.
Doctor: How about the ones I gave you earlier?
Patient: Those pills gave me diarrhoea.
Doctor: Hmm…..maybe you should take **one of each.**

A man asks a trainer in the gym: "I want to **impress** that beautiful girl, which machine can I use?"

The trainer replied; **"Use the ATM outside the gym!!!"**

One blonde tells another: I've done pregnancy test.
Other blonde: And were the questions difficult?

❖

The speaker at the health forum asked the audience, "What food causes the most suffering for years, after eating it?"
After a long silence an old man answered, **"The wedding cake."**

❖

Angry husband to wife: I have to take a bath. Make the water hot. **Otherwise......**
Wife's angry response: Otherwise what will you do?
Husband's meek reply: Otherwise I will take a bath **with cold water**.

❖

Marriage & Newlyweds

After marriage, husband and wife become two sides of a coin; they just can't face each other, but still they stay together.

"Honey," said the husband to his wife, "I invited a friend home for supper."

"What? Are you crazy? The house is a mess, I didn't go shopping, all the dishes are dirty, and I don't feel like cooking a fancy meal!"

"I know all that."

"Then, why did you invite a friend for supper?"

"Because the poor guy is thinking about getting married."

Marriage and love are both purely a matter of chemistry. That is why wives treat husbands like **toxic waste**.

At a wedding ceremony all were watching the radiant bride as her father escorted her down the aisle.

They reached the altar and the bride kissed her father and placed something in his hand. The father looked at the item and with great joy hugged and kissed his daughter.

Everyone in the room was wondering what was given to the father by the bride.

The father, feeling the suspense in the air, went to the mike and announced, "Ladies and Gentlemen, today is the luckiest day of my life."

Then he raised his hands to show what his daughter gave him and continued, "My daughter **finally, finally returned my credit card to me**."

The whole audience including the priest laughed………..**but not the poor groom!**

Before marriage, a man will lie awake all night listening to her till she finishes talking.

After marriage, he will fall asleep **before she starts.**

There was this guy who told his woman that he loved her so much that he would go through hell for her.

They got married and now **he is going through hell.**

❖

At the start of a married life, every woman treats her husband as **GOD.**

Later on, somehow, the alphabets get **reversed**……

❖

Man: Is there any way for long life?
Doctor: Get married.
Man: Will it help?
Doctor: No, but the thought of long life will **never come.**

❖

**After marriage, we always hold hands.
If I let go, she shops.**

❖

Son: Why do couples hold hands during their wedding?

Father: It's a formality just like two boxers shaking hands before the fight begins!

If you are married please ignore this message; for everyone else:
 "Happy Independence Day"

The shortest story ever told:
Once upon a time, a guy asked a girl:
 "Will you marry me?"
 She said: "No."
 And he lived happily ever after.
 THE END

Trouble in marriage often starts when a man gets so busy earning his salt that he forgets his sugar.

A woman complained to her marriage counsellor about her husband's selfishness.

"When he won a trip for two to Hawaii, **he went twice.**"

Marriage is an agreement in which a man loses his bachelor degree and a woman gains her master.

It doesn't matter …...how often a married man changes his job! He still ends up **with the same boss.**

Marriage is a relationship in which…..one person is always right! and… **the other is a husband.**

❖

Two secrets to keep your marriage brimming.
1. Whenever you're wrong, **admit it**,
2. Whenever you're right, **shut up**.

❖

Yawn: The only time some married men ever get to open their mouth.

❖

For Sale:
      Wedding dress, size 8.
      Worn once by mistake.

❖

Marriage is **grand** -- and divorce is at least **100 grand!**

❖

The wise never marry, and when they marry they become **otherwise**.

❖

It's funny when people discuss Love Marriage vs. Arranged Marriage.
It's like asking someone, **if suicide is better or being murdered.**

❖

Don't marry for money; you can **borrow it cheaper.**
--Scottish Proverb

❖

I don't worry about **terrorism**. I was married for two years.
--Sam Kinison

❖

I never married because I have three pets at home that serve the same purpose as a husband. I have a **dog that growls** in the morning, **a parrot that swears** all afternoon, and a **cat that comes home late** at night.

- *Marie Corelli*

Marriage is the only war where one **sleeps with the enemy.**

People say that there is no difference between **'finished' and 'complete'**.
I say there is.....
Marry the right person, and you're **'complete'**.
Marry the wrong person, and you're **'finished'**.

Bachelor: A rolling stone that gathers no **miss.**

Wedding Anniversaries

Two elderly guys met after a long time.

One asked the other, "Roy, how are you going to celebrate your Golden Anniversary coming soon?"

The old guy pondered this for a moment, then replied, "For our 25th anniversary, I took my wife to China. For our 50th, I'm thinking about going down there again **to pick her up.**"

On anniversaries, the wise husband always forgets the past - but never the **present**.

Wife: Darling, today is our anniversary, what should we do?
Husband: Let us stand in **silence** for 2 minutes.

The most impressive evidence of tolerance is a golden wedding anniversary.

A married couple, both 60 years old, were celebrating their 35th anniversary. During their party, a fairy appeared to congratulate them and grant them each one a wish.
The wife wanted to travel around the world. The fairy waved her wand and poof -- the wife had tickets in her hand for a world cruise.
Next, the fairy asked the husband what he wanted. He said, "I wish I had a wife 30 years younger than me."
So the fairy picked up her wand and poof -- **the husband was 90**.

Grandpa and his wife were discussing their 50th wedding anniversary when she said, "Shall I kill a chicken tonight?"
"Naw," said Grandpa, "**Why blame a bird** for something that happened 50 years ago."

Husbands & Wives

A woman's husband dies. He had $20,000 to his name. After the funeral, she tells her closest friend that there is no money left.

The friend says, "How can that be? You told me he had $20,000 a few days before he died."

The widow says, "Well, the funeral and service expenses came to $2,500 and the rest went for the memorial stone."

The friend says, "$17,500 for the memorial stone? My God, how big was it?"

The widow says, **"Three carats."**

❖

Wife: Let's go out and have some fun tonight.

Husband: Okay, but if you get home before I do, **leave the hall light on**.

❖

The husband asked the wife, "Darling if anything happens to me and I die, will you marry again."

The wife replied, "No, of course not, Dear. I will just go and stay with my sister."

The wife then asked the husband, "And how about you Darling, if anything happens to me and I die, will you marry again?"

"No, Dear." replied the husband, **"I will also go and stay with your sister."**

❖

When I got my first grandchild and became a grandfather, I had **mixed** feelings.

I was happy I was a grandfather but then I had to **sleep with a grandmother**.

❖

Always listen to your wife, she gives sound advice.

99% sound & 1% advice!

❖

The husband bought his wife an electric blender, electric toaster, and electric bread maker.

Then she said, "There are too many gadgets, and no place to sit down!"

So the husband bought her an **electric chair**.

Jake was dying. His wife sat at the bedside.

He looked up and said weakly, "I have something I must confess."

"There's no need to," his wife replied.

"No," he insisted, "I want to die in peace. I slept with your sister, your best friend, her best friend, and your mother!"

"I know, I know," she replied. "Now just rest and **let the poison work**."

My wife and I always compromise. I admit I'm wrong and she agrees with me.

The position of a Husband is just like a Split Air Conditioner
No matter how loud he is in the **outdoor** He is designed to remain **Silent indoor...**

A woman was complaining to the neighbour that her husband always came home late, no matter how she tried to stop him.

"Take my advice," said the neighbour, "and do what I did. Once my husband came home at three o'clock in the morning, and from my bed I called out: "Is that you, Jim?" And that cured him.

"Cured him!" asked the woman, "but how?"

The neighbour said, **"His name is Bill."**

As seen on a car bumper:
"Driver does not carry cash. He is married"

A wife, one evening, drew her husband's attention to the couple next door and said, "Do you see that couple? How devoted they are? He kisses her every time they meet. Why don't you do that?"

"I would love to..." replied the husband. **"But I don't know her well enough."**

From his death bed, the husband called his wife and said, "One month after I die I want you to marry Samy."

"Samy! But he is your enemy!"

"Yes, I know that! I've suffered all these years **so let him suffer now."**

"Husband is one who is the **head** of the family, but his wife is the **neck**, and whichever way she turns, **he goes.**"

Why do most Indian women request God for the same husband in the next life?
Because her efforts taken to train him in this life **should not go to waste!**

❖

To be happy with a man, understand him a lot and love him a little.

To be happy with a woman, love her a lot and not try to understand her at all.

❖

Wife: Honey, what is inflation?

Husband: Earlier you were 36-24-36. Now you are 40-42-48. Now you have much more than before, yet your worth is much less. **That is inflation.**

❖

Ordeal of a bride

A young couple got married and left on their honeymoon. When they were back at home after a few days, the bride called her mother.

"Well, how was the honeymoon?" asked the mother.

"Oh, Mama," she replied, "the honeymoon was wonderful! So romantic..." Suddenly she burst out crying. "But, Mama, as soon as we returned, Sam started using the most horrible language. He's been saying things I've never heard before! All these awful **four-letter** words! You've got to come get me and take me home! Please, Mama!"

"Sarah, Sarah," her mother said, "calm down! Tell me, what could be so awful? What four-letter words has he been using?"

"Please don't make me tell you, Mama," wept the daughter, "I'm so embarrassed! They're just too awful! You've got to come get me and take me home! Please, Mama!"

"Darling, baby, you must tell me what has made you so upset. Tell your mother these horrible **four-letter** words!"

Still sobbing, the bride replied, **"Oh, Mama ... words like cook, wash, iron, and dust..."**

An old man goes to the Wizard to ask him if he can remove a curse he has been living with for the last 40 years.
The Wizard says, "Maybe, but you will have to tell me the **exact** words that were used to put the curse on you."
The old man says without hesitation, **"'I now pronounce you man and wife.'"**

Wife: You delivered an excellent speech.
Husband: Thanks, dear, but the audience was full of fools and idiots.
Wife: Is that why you addressed them **as your brothers and sisters?**

A wife asked her husband: "What do you like most in me, my pretty face or my sexy body?"
He looked at her from head to toe and replied:
"I like **your sense of humour**!"

During a robbery, one of the robbers' mask slid down.
He looked at a man and asked. Did you see my face?
The man said yes! The robber shot him.
Then he asked a woman. Did you see my face?
She said **"No, but my husband over there did."**

The husband and wife were out to dinner one night. The waiter tells them the night's special is chicken almandine and fresh fish.
"The chicken sounds good; I'll have that," the woman says.
The waiter nods. "And the vegetable?" he asks.
The woman replied, **"Oh, he'll have the fish."**

If you want your wife to listen and pay strict attention to every word you say; talk in your sleep.

Keeping a mistress
A boss, in order to keep a mistress, bought a house in Shenzhen for her to live in.

The house cost him about 1 million Yuan.

After 5 years he sold the house for 3.2 million Yuan, after he broke off from his mistress.

A quick calculation revealed that after 5 years of free fling with the woman, he still had a net gain of 2.2 million Yuan.

Basking in his glory, he kept gloating over this episode. When his wife found out about this, she was very mad and gave him a big scolding: **"Why the hell did you just keep only one mistress!?"**

A man is stopped by the police at midnight and asked where he's going.

"I'm on the way to listen to a lecture about the effects of alcohol and drug abuse on the human body."

The policeman asks, "Really? And who's going to give a lecture at this time of night?"

"My wife", comes the reply.

Man: I want to share everything with you, my darling.
Woman: Let's start from **your bank account.**

One spelling mistake can destroy your life!

A husband sent an email to his wife on his business trip and forgot to add **'e'** at the end of a word...

"I am having such a wonderful time!
Wish you were **her**"

Husband: Do you know the meaning of W I F E? It means, '**W**ithout **I**nformation, **F**ighting **E**verytime!'
Wife: No, It means, '**W**ith **I**diot **F**or **E**ver!!!'

Wife: I had to marry you to find out how stupid you are.
Husband: You should have known it the minute I asked you to **marry me**.

❖

Husband: When I get mad at you, you never fight back. How do you control your anger?
Wife: Well, I just go and clean the toilet.
Husband: How does that help?
Wife: **I use your toothbrush.**

❖

Man comes home, finds his wife with his friend in bed. He shoots his friend to death.
Wife says, "If you behave like this, **you will lose ALL your friends**".

❖

Men and Women

Many girls like to marry a **military man** - he can cook, sew, and make beds and is in good health, and he's already **used to taking orders.**

❖

The woman said to her beautician as she sat down for her appointment, "When you're finished with me, will my husband think I'm beautiful?"

"Maybe," replied the beautician, **"does he still drink a lot?"**

❖

One woman told another: "My neighbour is always speaking ill of her husband, but look at me, my husband is foolish, lazy and a coward; but **have I ever said anything bad about him?"**

❖

Men are fools to marry women, but what else can they marry.

❖

No woman has ever shot her husband while he was doing the dishes.

❖

A German psychologist says that women talk more than men because they have a bigger vocabulary.
But, it evens out because men only listen half the time.
                                                    - Jay Leno

❖

An average woman can talk faster than any husband can listen.

❖

A married man is one who uses **both** hands to drive his car.

❖

A woman is happy if she has two things: **furniture** to move around, and a **husband** to move it around for her.

❖

The Reason Men Lie Is Because
Women Ask too Many Questions..

❖

A man can talk for hours on a topic but a woman can talk for hours **without any topic**.

❖

**Men are just like computers,
and a smart woman keeps a backup.**

❖

Q: Why are hurricanes normally named after women?
A: When they come, they're wild and wet, but when they go, they take your house and car with them.

Different phases of a man:

After engagement: Superman
After Marriage: Gentleman
After 10 years: Doorman
After 20 years: Doberman

There are two things men like women to do in a hurry. **Dress and Undress**!!

Woman inspires us to great things, and prevents us from achieving them.
... Dumas

Men are like Bananas. The older they get, the less firm they are.

❖

Men are like Government Bonds ....
They take soooooooo long to mature.

❖

The world's thinnest book has only one word written in it. **"Everything"**.
The book is titled: **"What Women Want!"**

❖

What does a man consider a **7- course meal**?
One hot dog and 6 cans of beer.

❖

Man's troubles are due to three things: women, money and **both**.

❖

Running after women never hurt anybody. It's the catching that does the damage.

❖

There are only two men in the world that understand women. One is dead and the other is crazy.

❖

**All men are created free and equal;
then they grow up and get married.**

❖

Prospective husband: Do you have a book called **, 'Man, The Master of Women'**?
Sales girl: The **fiction** department is on the other side, sir.

❖

A woman said to her friend, "Who is your favourite writer?"
"My husband," her friend said.
"What does he write?"
"Cheques".

❖

Men vs. Women

Smart man + Smart Woman = **Romance**
Smart Man + Dumb Woman = **Pregnancy**
Dumb Man + Smart Woman = **Affair**
Dumb Man **+ Dumb** Woman = **Marriage**

❖

Men should be like Kleenex; soft, strong and **disposable.** - Cher

Woman at various ages.

At 18 she is like a **football**. 22 men running after her.

At 28 she is like a **basketball**. 14 men running after her.

At 38 she is like a **golf ball**. 1 man chasing her.

At 48 she is like a **table tennis ball**. One man passing her to the other man.

At 58 and beyond, she is like a **mothball. Kept in the closet.**

Q What is the difference between men and government bonds?
A. The bonds mature.

Q. What do you call a woman who knows where her husband is every night?
A. A widow.

❖

A woman gets married to make two people happy**: herself and her mother**.

❖

Q: What is the difference between men and pigs?
A: Pigs don't turn into men when they **drink...**

❖

Q: What did God say after he created man?
A: I can do better than this! And then He created woman!

❖

Men Vs. Women

MAN:
1) Pull up to ATM machine
2) Wind window down
3) Insert card, enter PIN
4) Retrieve cash
5) Drive away

WOMAN:
1) Pull up to ATM machine
2) Open door (too far away from machine)
3) Search through all of the 112 compartments in handbag for ATM card
4) Do make up, apply lipstick, fix hair
5) Insert Card
6) Remove card
7) Insert card the correct way up
8) Search for piece of paper with PIN on it
9) Enter PIN
10) Enter correct PIN
11) Retrieve cash, put in bag
12) Drive off
13) Reverse back to machine
14) Retrieve card
15) Drive three miles away
16) Release hand-brake

Fastest ways of communication
Three fastest means of communication in the world are:
Tele-phone
Tele-vision
Tell-a-woman.

You still want faster?
(**Tell her not to tell anyone**)

Man said to God --- Why did you make women so beautiful?
God said to man --- So that **you** will love them.
Man said to God --- But why did you make them so dumb?
God said to man --- So that **they** will love you.

Salesman: Lady, this vacuum cleaner will cut your work in half.
Housewife: Good. I'll take **two of them**.

**It is difficult to understand GOD.
He makes such beautiful things as women.....
and then He turns them into Wives !?!!!?!**

❖

A woman was in a gambling casino for the first time.
At the roulette table she says, "I have no idea what number to play."
A young, good-looking man nearby suggests she play her age.
Smiling at the man, she puts her money on number 32.
The wheel is spun, and 41 comes up.
The smile drifted from the woman's face and **she fainted.**

Girl to her boyfriend: One kiss and I'll be yours forever.
The guy replies: **Thanks for the early warning.**

Mothers – in – law

I'm thinking about getting married. I looked up the word **"engaged"** in the dictionary. It said, "To do battle with the enemy."

Then I looked up mother-in-law. It said**, "See engaged."**

Q: Under law, what is the maximum penalty for bigamy?

A: Two mothers-in-law.

A mother in law during her holidays in Australia went for a swim and was bitten by a great white shark.

The Hospital Doctors, Nurses and staff worked 24 hours day and night and did the best they could but the **poor shark died**.

One friend to another: Your mother-in-law is a real treasure.
Other friend replied: Yes, but I wish she was a **buried treasure**.

A guy was out shopping when he saw six women beating his mother-in-law up.
As he stood there and watched, his neighbour said, "Well, aren't you going to help?"
The guy replied, "No. **Six of them are enough**".

Then there was this guy who was told by his doctor that he has only 6 months to live.
He decided to move in with his mother-in-law, because living with her for 6 months will seem **like forever**.

SHE: This wine is described as full bodied and imposing with a nutty base, a sharp bite, and a bitter aftertaste.
HE: Are you describing the wine **or your mother?**

I bought my Mother-in-law an electric massage chair for Christmas, but she **did not dare to plug it in.**

A guy went for car shopping, and the salesman asked if he wanted a car with an **Airbag**.
The guy replied, "No thanks. **I already have a Mother-in-law."**

I always know when it's the mother-in-law knocking at the door – **the mice throw themselves into the traps.**

A guy brings his dog into the vet and says, "Could you please **cut my dog's tail off**?"

The vet examines the tail and says, "There is nothing wrong. Why would you want this done?"

The man replies, "My Mother-in-law is coming to visit, and I don't want **anything in the house to make her think that she is welcome!**"

A guy took his mother-in-law to Madame Tussaud's chamber of horrors and one of the attendants said, "Keep **her moving** sir, we're stocktaking."

God said, "I cannot be everywhere, so I created mother".

Devil replied, "Even I cannot be everywhere, so I created **mother-in-law!!**"

Husband and wife had a tiff. The wife called up her mum and said, "Mom, he fought with me again, I am coming to live with you".

Mom replied, "No, no sweetheart, he must pay for his mistake, **I am coming to stay with you.**"

A mother- in- law was kidnapped and they sent a piece of her finger to her son in law.

The guy replied he **wanted more proof**.

"I heard that your mother-in-law was dangerously ill last week."

"Yes, but this week she is **dangerously well again.**"

We had a **blessed event** at our house – my mother–in–law **finally left**.

A woman had 3 daughters, all married. One day she decided to test her sons-in-law. She invites the first one for a stroll by the lakeshore, purposely falls in and pretends to be drowning. Without any hesitation, the son-in-law jumps in and saves her.

The next morning, he finds a brand new car in his driveway with the message on the windscreen, "Thank you! Your mother- in- law loves you!"

A few days later, the lady does the same thing with the second son-in-law. He jumps in the water and save her also.

The next morning, he too finds a brand new car in his driveway with the message, "Thank you! Your mother- in- law loves you!"

A few days later she does the same thing with her third son-in-law. While she is drowning, the son-in-law looks at her without moving an inch and thinks, "Finally, it's about time that this old witch dies!"

The next morning he receives a brand new sports car with the message, **"Thank you! Your Father-in-law!"**

Age Matters

The secret to long life

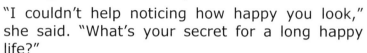

A woman walked up to a little old man rocking in a chair on his porch.

"I couldn't help noticing how happy you look," she said. "What's your secret for a long happy life?"

"I smoke three packs of cigarettes a day," he said. "I also drink a case of whiskey a week, eat fatty foods, and never exercise."

"That's amazing," said the woman, "how old are you?"

"Twenty-six," he said.

Doctor: Well, I have good news and bad news…
Patient: Come on, Doc. What's the bad news?
Doctor: You have Alzheimer's disease.
Patient: Good heavens! What's the good news?
Doctor: You can go home and **forget about it!**

Two elderly guys were sitting on the bench when one says to the other.

"Bill, I'm 73 years old now and I'm just full of aches and pains. I know you're about my age. How do you feel?"

Bill says, "I feel just like a newborn baby."

"Really? Like a newborn baby?"

"Yep. No hair, no teeth and I think I just wet my pants."

When Dan found out he was going to inherit a fortune when his sickly father died, he decided he needed a woman to enjoy it with.

So one evening he went to a singles bar where he spotted the most beautiful woman he had ever seen.

"I may look like just an ordinary man," he said as he walked up to her, "but in just a week or two, my father will die, and I'll inherit 20 million dollars."

Impressed, the woman went home with him that evening and, three days later, she became his **stepmother**.

An old man, 95, walks into a bar, sits down, and starts crying.

The bartender asks, "What's wrong?"

The old man looks at the bartender and between sobs says, "I married a beautiful woman two days ago. She's a natural blonde, twenty-five, intelligent, a marvellous cook, a great housekeeper, and intensely passionate in bed."

The bartender stares at the old man for a brief moment and says, "But that sounds great! You have what every man wants in a woman, so why are you crying?"

The old man looks at the bartender and says, **"I can't remember where I live!"**

Old man (80 year): My 28 year old wife is pregnant, your opinion Doctor?

Doctor: Let me tell you a story. A hunter in a hurry grabs an umbrella instead of the gun. He moves into the jungle, sees a lion, lifts the umbrella, pulls the handle and BANG... The lion drops dead!

Old man: That's impossible; someone else must have shot the lion.

Doctor: MY POINT EXACTLY!

WHO SAYS OLD FOLKS AREN'T WORTH ANYTHING

Take heart! We are more valuable than any of the younger generations:
1   We have **silver** in our hair;
2   We have **gold** in our teeth;
3   We have **stones** in our kidneys;
4   We have **lead** in our feet;
5   We are loaded with **natural gas**.

An 85 year old man got married to a 15 year old girl. On their first night, both were crying. Why? Because she didn't know anything: and he had forgotten everything.

I am so old that whenever I eat out they ask me for money up front!!

Two old friends met by chance on the street. After chatting for some time one said to the other, "I'm terribly sorry, but I've forgotten your name. You'll need to tell me".

The other stared at him thoughtfully for a long time, then replied, **"How soon do you need to know?"**

❖

There are three signs of old age. The first is your loss of memory. I forget the other two.

❖

Poor old Bob looking for love sent his picture to the Lonely Hearts Club.

The reply came back, "We are **not that lonely**."

❖

**One good thing about Alzheimers....
You get to meet new people everyday.**

❖

Two elderly couples were enjoying friendly conversation when one of the men asked the other, "Fred, how was the memory clinic you went to last month?"

"Outstanding," Fred replied. "They taught us all the latest psychological techniques: visualization, association, etc. It was great."

"That's great! And what was the name of the clinic?"

Fred went blank. He thought and thought, but couldn't remember. Then a smile broke across his face and he asked, "What do you call that flower with the long stem and thorns?"

"You mean a rose?"

"Yes, that's it!" He turned to his wife, **"Rose, what was the name of that memory clinic?"**

My Grandmother is over eighty and still doesn't need glasses.

Drinks right out of the bottle.

Henny Youngman

An old lady approached a young man browsing in the supermarket. "Pardon me, but you resemble so much like my son who recently passed away."

"I'm very sorry," replied the young man, "is there anything I can do for you?"

"Yes," she said, "As I'm leaving, can you say 'Good bye, Mother'? It would make me feel so much better."

"Sure," answered the young man.

As the old woman was leaving, he called out, "Goodbye, Mother!"

As he stepped up to the checkout counter, he saw that his total was $127.50.

"How can that be?" He asked, "I only purchased a few things!"

"Your mother said that you would pay for her," said the clerk.

Three old guys are out walking.
First one says, "Windy, isn't it?"
Second one says, "No, it's Thursday!"
Third one says, "So am I. Let's go get a beer."

At 85 years of age, Morris married Lou Anne, a lovely 25 year old.

Since her new husband is so old, Lou Anne decides to sleep in a separate bedroom, because she is concerned that her aged husband may over exert himself if they spend the entire night together.

As she goes to bed she hears a knock on the door. Sure enough there is Morris, her 85 year old groom, ready for action.

They unite as one. All goes well, Morris takes leave of his bride, and she goes to sleep.

After a few minutes, Lou Anne hears another knock on her bedroom door. Morris is back again, and is as fresh as a 25-year-old, ready for more "action" and once again they enjoy each other.

But as Morris gets set to leave again, his young bride says to him, "I am impressed that at your age you can perform so well **twice**. You are truly a great lover, Morris."

Morris, somewhat embarrassed, turns to Lou Anne and says: **"You mean I have been here already?"**

The moral of the story:
Don't be afraid of getting old. **Alzheimer's has its advantages.**

An 80 years old man marries a girl who is 20.
After a year of marriage she went into the hospital to give birth. The nurse came out to congratulate the old fellow saying "This is amazing! How do you do it at your age?"

He answered, "You've got to keep the old motor running."

The following year the young bride gave birth again.

The same nurse said, "You're amazing, how do you do it?"

He again said "You've got to keep the old motor running".

The same thing happened the third year.

The old man tells the same nurse, "See, you've got to keep the old motor running."

The nurse said, **"Well, you better change the oil, this one is black!"**

Did you hear about the 95 year – old who married a woman of 90?

They spent the entire honeymoon **getting out of the car.**

It's good to be old

A woman spent $5,000 and got a face lift for her birthday. She felt really good about the result. On her way home she went into McDonalds for lunch, and asked the order – taker, "How old do you think I am?"

"About 27," was the reply.

"I'm actually 47," the woman said, feeling really happy.

While standing at the bus stop she asked an old man the same question. He replied, "I am 85 years old and my eyesight is going. But when I was young there was a sure way of telling a woman's age. If I put my hand over your blouse I will be able to tell your exact age."

As there was no one around, the woman thought, "Well, let him try", and she let him feel over her blouse.

After feeling around for a while, the old man said, "Ok, You are 47."

Stunned the woman said, "That was brilliant! How did you do that?"

The old man replied, **"I was behind you in line at McDonalds!"**

DON'T MESS WITH SENIORS!!!

A woman went to breakfast at a restaurant where the **"seniors' special"** was two eggs, bacon, hash browns and toast for $1.99.

"Sounds good," said the woman. "But I don't want the eggs."

"Then I will have to charge you two dollars and forty-nine cents because you're ordering a-la-carte," the waitress warned her.

"You mean I'd have to pay for not taking the eggs?" asked the woman.

"YES!!" stated the waitress.

"In that case I'll take the special." Said the woman.

"How do you want your eggs?" the waitress asked.

The woman replied, "Raw and in the shell."

She took the two eggs home.

Two elderly women boarded a plane for their first flight and approached the pilot. "Now, young man," said one, "don't fly faster than sound. **We want to talk.**"

A tour bus driver is driving with a bus load of seniors down a highway when he is tapped on his shoulder by a little old lady. She offers him a handful of peanuts, which he gratefully munches up.

After about 15 minutes, she hands him another handful of peanuts.

She repeats this gesture about five more times.

When she is about to hand him another batch again, he asks the little old lady, 'Why don't you eat the peanuts yourself?'

'We can't chew them because we've no teeth,' she replied.

The puzzled driver asks, 'Why do you buy them then?'

The old lady replied, **'We just love the chocolate around them.'**

As a senior citizen was driving down the freeway, his car phone rang. Answering, he heard his wife's voice urgently warning him, "Herman, I just heard on the news that there's a car going the wrong way on Interstate 77. Please be careful!"

"Heck," said Herman, "It's not just one car. **It's hundreds of them!"**

Family life – Parents & Kids

A young child walked up to her mother and sweetly asked; "Mom, Why do you have some grey strands in your hair?"

The mother looked at her daughter and said, "Well, every time that you do something wrong and make me cry or unhappy, one of my hairs turns white."

The little girl stood there thinking, and sweetly asked again, "**Mother, then how come all of Grandma's hairs are white?**"

A little girl was watching her parents dress for a party. When she saw her dad donning his tuxedo, she warned, "Daddy, you shouldn't wear that suit."

"And why not, darling?"

"You know that it always gives you a **headache the next morning.**"

The happy father stood watching his teenage son mow the lawn.

Mother: How did you manage to do that?
Father: I told him I lost the car keys in the grass.

❖

Susan: My mother started dieting last month.
Liza: Did she lose anything?
Susan: Yes, everyday she loses her temper.

❖

Office: A place where you can relax after your strenuous **home life**.

❖

Teacher: Children tell me who has better eyesight, a human or a bird?
Student: Sir, a bird.
Teacher: Why?
Student: Sir, have you seen a bird wearing glasses?

❖

On the first day of college, the Dean addressed the students:

"The female dormitory is out-of-bounds for all male students, and the male dormitory to the female students. Anybody caught breaking this rule will be fined $20 the first time, $60.00 the second time and the third time will cost you a fine of $180. Are there any questions?"

A male student inquired, "How much for a season pass?"

They call our language the mother tongue because the father seldom gets to speak.

Two boys were bragging about the abilities of their mothers.

"I'll bet my mama can talk one hour on **any subject**." Said one.

"Huh!" replied the other fellow proudly. "My mama **can talk one hour without a subject**."

Mother to her teenage daughter: I think this is the right time we should talk about sex.
Daughter (Excitingly): Sure mom, tell me what do you want to know.
Mother Faints...

Teacher: I wish you would pay a little attention!
Student: I am paying as **little** as I can, Sir!

The father of five children had won a toy at a raffle. He called his kids together to ask which one should have the present.

"Who is the most obedient?" He asked. "Who never talks back to mother?" "Who does everything she says?"

Five small voices answered in union. **"Okay, dad, you get the toy."**

Teacher: Peter, why are you late for school again?
Peter: Well, Miss, I dreamt that I was playing football and the **game went into extra time**.

Teacher: Ted, if your father has $10 and you ask him for $6, how much would your father still have?
Ted: $10.
Teacher: You don't know maths.
Ted: **You don't know my father!**

Mother: David, come here.
David: Yes, mum?
Mother: You really disappoint me. Your results are getting worse.
David: But I will only get my report book tomorrow.
Mother: I know that. But I am going to China tomorrow, **so I am scolding you now.**

Father: Why did you fail your mathematics test?
Son: On Monday, teacher said 3+5=8
Father: So?
Son: On Tuesday, she said 4+4=8. And on Wednesday, she said 6+2=8. If she can't make up her mind, **how do I know the right answer?**

❖

Girl: Do you love me?
Boy: Yes Dear
Girl: Would you die for me?
Boy: No, **mine is undying love.**

❖

Teacher: Simon, your composition on "My Dog" is exactly the same as your brother's. Did you copy his?
Simon: No, teacher, **it's the same dog!**

❖

Father: Your teacher says she finds it impossible to teach you anything!
Son: That's why I say **she's no good!**

Teacher: Where were you born?
Student: India, Sir.
Teacher: Which part?
Student: **All of me, Sir.**

Little Johnny: Dad, I want to get married.
Father: Oh, so do you have someone special in your mind?
Johnny: Yes…Grandma
Father: What? There is a problem now; you want to marry my Mother?
Johnny: Why not? **You married my mother.**

A man asked the barber "How much for a haircut?"

"$10.00," said the barber.

"And how much for a shave?"

"$3.00 sir."

"Very well, shave my head."

Father: (to son after exam) Son, let me see your report card.

Son: My friend just borrowed it. **He wants to scare his parents.**

During a blackout:
Johnny: Dad, can you write in the dark?
Dad: Of course, I can.
Johnny: Good, please sign my report card.

Teacher: Rina, what is your favourite flower?
Rina: Chrysanthemums.
Teacher: Spell it.
Rina: Actually come to think of it, I like **roses better.**

The boy was filling An Application form….
The form asked about "Mother Tongue"?
Son: Dad, what do I write here?
Dad: Son, write here, **"VERY LONG AND UNCONTROLLED"**

Teacher: Why are you always late for school?
Student: Because you always **ring the bell before I get here!**

Teacher: Why is your homework in your Dad's writing?
Johnny: I used **his pen**.

Little Susie came running into the house after school one day, shouting,
"Daddy! Daddy! I got a 100 in school today!"
"That's great, Sweetheart," said her daddy.
"Come in to the living room and tell me about it."
"Well," began the confession, "I got **50** in spelling, **30** in maths and **20** in science."

A Sunday school teacher asked her little children, as they were on the way to church service, "And why is it necessary to be quiet in church?"
One bright little girl replied, **"Because people are sleeping."**

After her first lesson in zoology, the high school girl came home and asked her mother, "Is it true, mother, that I am descended from an ape?"
"I am not sure," her mother said, **"I don't know your father's people very well."**

You Know Your kids Have Grown Up When:
Your Daughter Begins To **Put On Lipstick.....**
Or when your Son starts **to wipe it off.**

❖

Teacher: What are some products of the West Indies?
Student: I don't know.
Teacher: Of course, you do. Where do you get sugar from?
Student: We borrow it from our neighbour.

❖

Jimmy (studying history)**:** Grandpa, do you know what Great War broke out in 1939?
Grandpa: Why, that was the **year I married your grandmother.**

❖

A: I have the perfect son.
B: Does he smoke?
A: No, he doesn't.
B: Does he drink whiskey?
A: No, he doesn't.
B: Does he ever come home late?
A: No, he doesn't.
B: I guess you really do have the perfect son. How old is he?
A: He will be **six months old** next Wednesday.

A 6 year-old to his teacher:

My dad thinks he wears the **pants** in our house, but it's mom who tells him **which pair** to put on.

Little Johnny: Teacher, can I go to the bathroom?
Teacher: Johnny, **MAY** I go to the bathroom?
Little Johnny: But I asked first!

Teacher: Johnny, why are you doing your math multiplication on the floor?
Johnny: You told me to do it **without using tables**.

Teacher: Now, you must not say, "I ain't goin'." You should say, "I am not going, he is not going; we are not going; they are not going."
Student: Wow! **Ain't nobody goin' then?**

Sam: Dad, would you do my math homework for me?
Dad: No, son, it wouldn't be right.
Sam: Well, at least **you could try**.

A Will
A rich man died and a line in his will read, **"I leave to my beloved son all the money he owes me."**

DOCTORS & PATIENTS

A guy phones a dentist to enquire about the cost for a tooth extraction.

"$50.00 for an extraction, sir" the dentist replied.

"$50.00!! That's a lot. What about if you use one of your dentist trainees and don't use any anaesthetic?"

"That's unusual, sir. I can't guarantee their professionalism and it'll be painful. But the price could drop to $20.00".

"How about if you make it a training session, and get your student to do the extraction with the other students watching and learning?"

It'll be good for the students", said the dentist. "It's going to be very traumatic, but I'll charge you $5.00."

"Ah! That's what I like! It's a deal," said the guy. **"Can you confirm an appointment for my wife next Tuesday then?"**

A Doctor is a person who kills your ills by pills, and then kills you **with his bills**.

Patient: Doctor, Doctor, if I take these green pills, will I get better?

Doctor: Well, nobody I've given them to has ever come back.

❖

A young woman went to her doctor complaining of pain.

"Where does it hurt?" asked the doctor.

"I hurt all over", said the woman.

"What do you mean, all over?" asked the doctor, "be a little more specific."

The woman touched her right knee with her index finger and yelled, "Ow, that hurts." Then she touched her left cheek and again yelled, "Ouch! That hurts, too." Then she touched her right earlobe, "Ow, even THAT hurts", she cried.

The doctor checked her thoughtfully for a moment and told her his diagnosis, **"You have a broken finger."**

❖

God heals – the doctor takes the fees.

❖

A man consults a therapist and states, "Doc, I'm suicidal. What should I do?"

The doctor replies **"Pay in advance."**

After the heart transplant the doctor advised the patient to have sex only with his wife.

"Why?" asked the patient.

Doctor: **To avoid excitement.**

"Doctor, you must help me. I swallowed a gold coin ten years ago." Said the man.

"Good heavens!" said the Doctor. "Why didn't you seek help before?"

"I didn't need the money then." Said the man.

Confucius say: Man who want pretty nurse, must be **patient**.

A man who had come out of a complicated abdominal surgery was complaining of having a bump on his head and a terrible headache.

The nurse spoke to the surgeon about it. The doctor assured the nurse, "don't worry about a thing. He has a bump on his head because **halfway into the operation we ran out of anaesthetic."**

Nurse: Good morning Mr. Smith, you seem to be coughing much more easily this morning.
Mr. Smith: That's because I've been practicing all night.

Doctor: Your husband needs rest and peace. Here are some sleeping pills.
Wife: When must I give them to him?
Doctor: **They are for you**.

A nurse found one elderly gentleman – already dressed and sitting on the bed with a suitcase at his feet – who insisted he didn't need her help to leave the hospital.

After a chat about rules being rules, he reluctantly let her wheel him to the elevator. On the way down, she asked if his wife was meeting him.

"I don't know," he said. **"She's still upstairs in the bathroom changing out of her hospital gown."**

Maurice an 82 year-old man went to the doctor for his physical check-up.

A few days later the doctor saw Maurice walking down the street with a gorgeous young lady on his arm.

A couple of days later the doctor spoke to Maurice and said, "You're really doing great, aren't you?"

Maurice replied, "Just doing what you said, Doc: "Get a hot mamma and be cheerful."

The doctor said, "I did not say that. I said, **"You got a heart murmur. Be careful."**

Doctor: What's wrong with your brother?
Boy: He thinks he is a chicken.
Doctor: Really? How long has this been going on?
Boy: Five years.
Doctor: Five years! Why didn't you bring him earlier?
Boy: We would have, but **we needed the eggs**.

This paediatrician asked six-year-old Johnny, who watched a good many TV ads, just to make conversation. "Johnny, if you found a couple of dollars and had to spend them, what would you buy?"

"A box of tampons," he replied without hesitation.

"Tampons?" said the doctor. "What would you do with that?"

"Well," said Johnny, "With tampons, it says on TV, you can go swimming, go horseback riding, and also go skating, any time you want to. **It sure is worth two dollars.**"

A woman goes to the pharmacy and tells the pharmacist that she wanted to buy some cyanide to poison her husband.

The pharmacist's eyes got big and he said, "Lord, have mercy – I can't give you cyanide to kill your husband! That's against the law! I'll lose my license; they'll throw both of us in jail. No I am sorry, you CANNOT have any cyanide!"

The lady reached into her purse and pulled out a picture of her husband in bed with the pharmacist's wife.

The pharmacist looked at the picture and replied, **"Well, now. You didn't tell me you had a prescription."**

A patient consults the doctor and said "I am thinking about getting a vasectomy."

"That's a pretty big decision. Have you talked it over with your family?" the doctor asks.

"Yes, I have," answers the man.

"Well, what did they have to say about it?" the doctor asks.

The man replies, **"They're in favour, 10 to 2."**

"Doctor, Doctor, You've got to help me – I just can't stop my hands shaking!"
"Do you drink a lot?"
"Not really – **I spill most of it**!"

At a funeral, a guy noticed that the deceased's coffin was in the **shape of a heart**.
"Why the heart shape?" he enquired.
"He is a cardiologist – a Heart specialist."
The guy gave a worried look and exclaimed, "Oh, my God!"
"Why, what are you so worried about?"
"I am visualising the shape of my coffin."
"Why, what is your profession?"
"I am a **gynaecologist**."

Patient: How much to have this tooth pulled?
Dentist: $100.00.
Patient: $100.00 for just a few minutes work?
Dentist: Well, I can extract it very slowly if you like.

Patient: What are the chances of my recovering Doc?
Doctor: One hundred percent. Medical records show that nine out of ten people die of the disease you have. Yours is the tenth case I've treated; **the others all died**.

Patient: Doc, I have an unusual disease. Whenever my wife speaks I am **unable** to hear her.
Doctor: This is not a disease. This is a **blessing to you from God.**

Two doctors were chatting over a cup of coffee.
1st Doctor: I just operated on a lady, and in the nick of time, too.
2nd Doctor: Oh Really?
1st Doctor: Yeah; another day and she would have **recovered without the operation.**

A guy went to the psychiatrist and told him, 'I've got problems. Every time I go to bed I think there's somebody under it. I'm scared. I think I'm going crazy…'

'Just put yourself in my hands for one year,' said the psychiatrist. 'Come talk to me three times a week and we should be able to get rid of those fears.'

'How much do you charge?'

'Eighty dollars per visit,' replied the doctor.

'I'll sleep on it,' he said.

Six months later the psychiatrist met this guy on the street.

'Why didn't you come to see me about those fears you were having?' he asked.

'Well, Eighty bucks a visit three times a week for a year is an awful lot of money! A bartender cured me for $10. I was so happy to have saved all that money that I went and bought myself a new car!'

'Is that so?' he said, 'and how, may I ask, did a bartender cure you?'

'He told me to cut the legs off the bed! – Ain't nobody under there now!!!'

DUMP THOSE PSYCHIATRISTS. GO HAVE A DRINK & TALK TO YOUR BARTENDER.

Woman Patient: Doc, Please call my husband inside.

Doctor: Don't worry. I am a gentleman.

Woman Patient: I know. **But your nurse is alone outside and my husband is not a gentleman.**

While visiting a friend in the hospital a young man noticed several pretty nurses, each one of them was wearing a pin designed to look like an **apple**.
 "What does the pin signify?" he asked one of them.
"Oh! Nothing," she said with a chuckle. "We just use it to **keep the doctors away**."

A psychiatrist's secretary walks into his study and says,
"There's a gentleman in the waiting room asking to see you. He claims he's invisible."
The psychiatrist responds, "Tell him **I can't see him.**"

❖

When I had my surgery, the doctor gave me a **local** anaesthetic.
I could not afford the **imported** kind.

Woman: Doc, how is it, that such a little hole in my tooth feels so big to my tongue?
Dentist: Well, you know how a woman's tongue **exaggerates.**

The patient shook his doctor's hand in gratitude and said, "Since we are the best of friends, I would not want to insult you by offering payment. But I would like for you to know that I had mentioned you in my will."

"That is very kind of you," said the doctor emotionally, and then added, "Can I see that prescription I just gave you? I'd like to **make a little change.**"

A new arrival, about to enter hospital, saw two white coated doctors searching through the flower beds.

"Excuse me," he said, "have you lost something?"

"No," replied one of the doctors. "We're doing a heart transplant for an **income-tax inspector** and want to **find a suitable stone**."

Patient: Well, doc, what does the X-ray of my head show?
Doctor: **Nothing.**

A psychiatrist is a person who will give you expensive answers that your wife will give you for **free**.

Patient: Doctor, I have a ringing in my ears.
Doctor: Don't answer!

Lawyers & Judges

A lawyer after listening critically to a potential client's story:

'Hmmm.... I don't think they can put you in prison for such a small thing.'

'Where do you think I'm calling from?'

❖

Judge to defendant: Have you anything to offer the court before sentence is passed on you?

Defendant: No, Your Honour. My lawyer took my last dollar.

❖

In the middle of a trial, the judge asks the defendant:
"You didn't bring your attorney today?"
"No, your honour, I've decided to **tell the truth**.

❖

Several women appeared in court, each accusing the others of causing the trouble they were having in the apartment building where they lived.

The women were arguing noisily, even in the courtroom.

The judge banged his gavel to quieten them and said, "We are going to do this in an orderly manner. I can't listen to all of you at once. I'll hear the oldest first."

The case was dismissed for lack of testimony.

A **pick-pocket** was pronounced guilty and sentenced to 8 months jail term with an option of $200 fine by the judge.

His defence lawyer knowing that his client could not pay the fine, pleaded with the judge asking;

"Your honour, my client can only afford $50, but **if you allow him a few minutes in the crowd ……"**

People Really Said These Things in Court

Q: Doctor, before you performed the autopsy, did you check for a pulse?
A: No.
Q: Did you check for blood pressure?
A: No.
Q: Did you check for breathing?
A: No.
Q: So, then it is possible that the patient was alive when you began the autopsy?
A: No.
Q: How can you be so sure, Doctor?
A: Because his brain was sitting on my desk in a jar.
Q: But could the patient have still been alive, nevertheless?
A: Yes, it is possible that he could have been alive and practicing law.

Q: What is your date of birth?
A: July fifteenth.
Q: What year?
A: Every year.

Q: This myasthenia gravis – does it affect your memory at all?
A: Yes.
Q: And in what ways does it affect your memory?
A: I forget.
Q: You forget. Can you give us an example of something that you've **forgotten?**

❖

Q: What was the first thing your husband said to you when he woke that morning?
A: He said, "Where am I, **Cathy**?"
Q: And why did that upset you?
A: My name is **Susan**.

❖

Q: Now doctor, isn't it true that when a person dies in his sleep, he doesn't know about it until the next morning?

❖

Q: Were you present when your picture was taken?

❖

Q: Was it **you** or your younger brother who was killed in the war?

❖

Q: Did he kill you?

❖

Q: How far apart were the vehicles at the time of the collision?

❖

Q: How many times have you committed suicide?

❖

Q: She had three children, right?
A: Yes.
Q: How many were boys?
A: None.
Q: Were there any girls?

❖

Q: You say the stairs went down to the basement?
A: Yes.
Q: And these stairs, did they go up also?

❖

Q: Mr. Slattery, you went on a rather elaborate honeymoon, didn't you?
A: I went to Europe, sir.
Q: And you took your new wife?
A: Yes
Q: How was your first marriage terminated?
A: By death.
Q: And by whose death was it terminated?

❖

Q: Can you describe the individual?
A: He was about medium height and had a beard.
Q: Was this a male, or a female?

❖

What Lawyers should never ask....

In a trial, a Southern small town prosecuting attorney called his first witness to the stand. The witness was a grand motherly, elderly woman.

He approached her and asked, "Mrs. Jones, do you know me?"

She responded, "Why, yes I do know you, Mr. Williams. I've know you since you were a young boy, and frankly; you're a big disappointment to me. You lie and you cheat on your wife. You think you're a big shot when you are nothing more than a two-bit paper pusher. Yes, I know you."

The Lawyer was stunned. Not knowing what else to do, he pointed across the room and asked, "Mrs. Jones, do you know the defence attorney?"

She again replied, "Why yes, I do. I've known Mr. Bradley since he was a youngster, too. He's lazy, bigoted and he has a drinking problem. His law practice is one of the worst in the entire state. Not to mention he cheated on his wife with three different women, one of them was your wife. Yes, I know him."

The defence attorney almost died.

The judge asked both counsellors to approach the bench, and in a very quiet voice, said, **"If either of you rascals asks her if she knows me, I'll throw you in jail for contempt."**

"Mr. Clark, I have reviewed this case very carefully", said the divorce Court Judge, "and I've decided to give your wife $775 a week,"

"That's very fair, your honour," the husband said. **"And every now and then I'll try to send her a few bucks myself."**

Lawyer: Didn't you suspect burglars had been in the house when you saw all the drawers pulled out and the contents scattered all over the floor?

Woman: No, I just thought my husband had been looking for a clean shirt.

3 questions most commonly asked by lawyers:

1. How much money do you have?
2. Where can you get more?
3. Do you have anything you can sell?

At the Pearly Gates, Churches

Two rabbis walk into a bank. While waiting in line, bank robbers storm inside, not only robbing the bank but also forcing the customers to hand over their own money and jewellery.

One rabbi slips something into the hand of the other rabbi.

"What is this?" the rabbi whispered.

The other rabbi replied, **"It's the fifty bucks I owe you."**

There are only two kinds of people in the world.

Those who wake up in the morning and say, **"Good morning, Lord,"**

And there are those who wake up in the morning and say, **"Good Lord, its morning."**

A lady dies in the operation room and soon finds herself standing before St. Peter.

"Are you sure that I'm due here, St. Peter?"

St. Peter looks carefully at the Book of Life and says: "Why, no, my good woman, you're not due here for 30 or 40 years!"

Suddenly, the lady wakes up in the O.R. fit and fine and is given a medical discharge.

The lady says: "Doctor, since I'm here and all prepped could you perhaps give me a face lift and remove all this flabbiness under my arms? And maybe give me a little tummy tuck.

A week later, she is walking across the hospital parking lot when she is hit and killed by a truck.

She goes again before St. Peter and she asks: "I thought you said I'm not due here for 30 or 40 years?"

St. Peter says: **"I didn't recognize you, my dear!"**

She sang in church last week and 150 people **changed** their religion.

The pastor preached about the beautiful kingdom of heaven and asked the congregation, "How many of you would like to go to heaven from here?"

Everybody raised up their hands except a little lad sitting just in front of him.

"Don't you want to go to heaven son?" he asked.

"My mother seriously warned me not to go anywhere from here, **but to come back home"** replied the boy.

Inner Peace

A guy followed the simple advice he read in a church article to find inner peace.

The article read…

"The way to find inner peace is to finish all the things you have started."

So he looked around the house to see all the things he had started and hadn't finished….

And before leaving the house the next morning he finished off a bottle of red wine, a bottle of white, the J&B scotch, some Cognac , some cheesecake and a box of chocolates.

You have no idea how good he felt…….

A drunk staggers into a Catholic Church; enters a confessional booth; sits down but says nothing.

The Priest coughs a few times to get his attention, but the drunk just sits there.

Finally, the Priest pounds three times on the wall.

The drunk mumbles: "Ain't no use knocking, man. **There's no paper on this side either!** "

A minister parked his car in a no-parking zone in a large city because he was short of time and couldn't find a space with a meter. Then he put a note under the windshield wiper that read:

"I have circled the block 10 times. If I don't park here, I'll miss my appointment. **Forgive us our trespasses.**"

When he returned, he found a ticket from a police officer along with this note, "I've circled this block for 10 years. If I don't give you a ticket I'll lose my job. **Lead us not into temptation.**"

The Preacher's Salary

There was a preacher whose wife was expecting a baby so he went to the congregation and asked for a raise.

After much consideration and discussion, they passed a rule that whenever the preacher's family expanded, so would his pay-check.

After 6 children, this started to get expensive and the congregation held a meeting to discuss the preacher's salary.

There was much yelling and bickering about how much the clergyman's additional children were costing the church.

Finally, the Preacher got up and spoke to the crowd, 'Children are a gift from God,' he said.

Silence fell on the congregation.

In the back of the room, a little old lady stood up and in her frail voice said, **'Rain is also a gift from God, but when we get too much, we wear raincoats.'**

And the congregation said, **'Amen'**!

What's the difference between people who pray in church and those who pray in casinos?
The ones in the casinos are serious.

Cheers!
Mother Superior called all the nuns together and said to them, "I must tell you all something. We have a case of gonorrhoea in the convent."
"Thank God," said an elderly nun at the back. **"I'm so tired of chardonnay."**

❖

Moe: My wife got me to believe in religion.
Joe: Really?
Moe: Yeah. **Until I married her I didn't believe in hell.**

❖

Paddy was driving down the street in a sweat because he had an important meeting and couldn't find a parking place. Looking up to heaven he said, 'Lord take pity on me. If you find me a parking place I will go to Mass every Sunday for the rest of my life and give up my Irish whiskey!'
Miraculously, a parking place appeared.
Paddy looked up again and said**, 'Never mind, I found one.'**

A distinguished young woman on a flight from Switzerland asked the Priest beside her, "Father, may I ask a favour?"

"Of course, what may I do for you?"

"Well, I bought an expensive woman's electronic **hair dryer** for my mother's birthday that is unopened and well over the Customs limits, and I'm afraid they'll confiscate it. Is there any way you could carry it through Customs for me? Under your robes, perhaps?"

"I would love to help you, dear, but I must warn you: I will not lie."

"With your honest face, Father, no one will question you."

When they got to Customs, she let the priest go ahead of her.

The official asked, "Father, do you have anything to declare?"

"From the top of my head down to my waist, I have nothing to declare."

The official thought this answer strange, so he asked, "And what do you have to declare from your waist to the floor?"

"I have a marvellous instrument designed to be used on a woman, but which is, to date, **unused**."

Roaring with laughter, the official said, "Go ahead, Father... **Next!**"

A preacher was standing at the pulpit giving his Sunday sermon when a note was passed to him.

The only word written on the sheet was **IDIOT**.

Looking up at the congregation, the preacher smiled and said: I have heard of men who write letters and forget to sign their names but this is the first time I see a man sign his name and **forget to write the letter**.

❖

HIGHER POWER
A Sunday school teacher said to her children, "We have been learning how powerful kings and queens were in Bible times, but there is a Higher Power. Can anybody tell me what it is?"

One child blurted out, **'Aces!'**

❖

God may have created man before woman, but there is always a rough draft before the **masterpiece**.

❖

UNANSWERED PRAYER

The preacher's 5 year-old daughter noticed that her father always paused and bowed his head for a moment before starting his sermon.

One day she asked him why. 'Well, Honey,' he began, proud that his daughter was so observant of his messages, 'I'm asking the Lord to help me preach a good sermon.'

'So, how come He doesn't?' she asked.

A husband comes home from church; he greets his wife and lifts her up. He then carries her around the house.

The wife was so surprised and asked, "Did the bishop preach about being **romantic**"?

The husband replied, **"No, he said 'we must carry our burdens and sorrows'."**

When I was young I used to pray for a bike, then I realized that God doesn't work that way, **so I stole a bike and prayed for forgiveness.**

Those wonderful Church Bulletins!

The Fasting & Prayer Conference includes meals.

The sermon this morning: 'Jesus walks on the Water.'
The sermon tonight: **'Searching for Jesus.'**

Ladies, don't forget the rummage sale. It's a chance to get rid of those things not worth keeping around the house. **Bring your husbands.**

Don't let worry kill you off – **let the Church help.**

Miss Charlene Mason sang 'I will not pass this way again,' giving obvious **pleasure** to the congregation.

For those of you who have children and don't know it, we have a nursery downstairs.

At the evening service tonight, the sermon topic will be 'What Is Hell?' Come early and listen to our choir practice.

Please place your donation in the envelope along with the deceased person you want remembered.

The church will host an evening of fine dining, super entertainment and gracious hostility.

Potluck supper Sunday at 5:00 PM – prayer and medication to follow.

The eighth-graders will be presenting Shakespeare's Hamlet in the Church basement Friday at 7 PM. The congregation is invited to attend this **tragedy**.

Weight Watchers will meet at 7 PM at the First Presbyterian Church. Please use large **double door** at the side entrance.

❖

Minister: Why don't you come to church now, Harry?
Harry: For three reasons. First I don't like your theology; second, I don't like your singing; and third **it was in your church I first met my wife**.

❖

A preacher is the only man who can keep women quiet for an hour.

❖

Business & Banks

It was the day of the **big sale**. A long line formed by 8:30, the opening time, in front of the store.

A small man pushed his way to the front of the line, only to be pushed back, amid loud and colourful curses. On the man's second attempt, he was punched square in the jaw, and knocked around a bit, and then thrown to the end of the line again. As he got up the second time, he said to the person at the end of the line...

"That does it! If they hit me one more time, I don't open the store!"

"Do you believe in life after death?" the boss asked one of his employees.

"Yes, sir," the clerk replied.

"That's good," the boss said. "After you left early yesterday to go to your grandmother's funeral, **she stopped in to see you.**"

This guy dreamt that he was stabbed to death. Upon waking up, he went to his Bank to withdraw all his savings.

When the Manager asked him the reason for withdrawal, he replied, "I dreamt I was stabbed to death and your sign outside says, **'We will make your dreams come true'.**"

One day a man asked, "God, what is a million years to you?"

God said, "a million years to me is only a **second**."

"Hmmm," the man wondered. Then he asked, "God, what is a million dollars worth to you?"

God said, "a million dollars to me is only a penny."

So the man said, "God, can I have a penny?"

And God cheerfully said, "Sure!!! .....**just a second.**"

**Running into debt doesn't bother me;
It's running into a creditor that's upsetting.**

A client entered a Slimming course shop and noticed in the signboard that a "B" course was cheaper than an "A" course.

He opted for the cheaper "B" course in which a pretty blonde appeared and said to him, "Now in this exercise, I want you to run after me. If you catch me you can have me."

The guy tried hard but failed, but perspired a lot. He then decided to try the expensive "A" for better fun.

In this exercise a big fat ugly guy came up to him and said, "Now, I want you to run as fast as you can. **If I catch you I will have you**."

What worries me most about the credit crunch is that if one of my checks is returned stamped **'insufficient funds'**, I won't know whether that refers to mine or **the bank's..**

"Young man, do you think you can handle a variety of work"

"I sure can. **I've had 10 different jobs in four months.**"

New Age investment definitions

BEAR MARKET: A 6 to 18-month period when the kids get no allowance, the wife gets no jewellery, and the husband gets no sex.

MOMENTUM INVESTING: The fine art of buying high and selling low.

VALUE INVESTING: The art of buying low and selling lower

P/E RATIO: The percentage of investors wetting their pants as the market keeps crashing.

STANDARD & POOR: Your life in a nutshell.

MARKET CORRECTION: The day after you buy stocks.

CASH FLOW: The movement your money makes as it disappears down the toilet.

INSTITUTIONAL INVESTOR: Someone who has owned equities for the last two years and who's now locked up long-term in a hospital.

The man charged into the jewellery shop, slammed his fists angrily on the showcase, removed a wristwatch from his pocket and shook it under the nose of the owner. "You said this watch would last me a lifetime," he yelled.

"Yeah," admitted the owner. "But you **looked pretty sick the day you bought it."**

Business:
The economy is getting so bad; the other day my ATM gave me an **IOU.**

A man walks past a beggar on the corner of the street where he works. The beggar holds out his one hand and the man drops a coin into his hand. One day the man walks past the beggar again and notices the beggar is holding hold out both his hands. He asks: "Why are you holding out both of your hands?"

The beggar replied, "You see sir, business is going so well I decided to **open another branch"**.

RESTAURANTS

Waiter: And how did you find your steak, sir?
Customer: Well, I just pushed aside a bean and **there it was!**

Sign in a Restaurant:
All Drinking Water In This Establishment Has been Personally Passed By The Manager

"Waiter, I'm so hungry I could eat a horse."
"You couldn't have come to a better place, sir."

A lonely stranger went into a deserted restaurant and ordered the breakfast special. When his order arrived, he looked up at the waitress and asked, "How about a kind word?"
The waitress leaned over and whispered, **"Don't eat the meat."**

GOLF

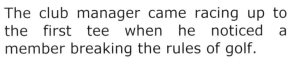

The club manager came racing up to the first tee when he noticed a member breaking the rules of golf.

"Oh, SIR...SIR!" The manager called out, "You're not allowed to tee off from there. You are a full 3 yards in front of the markers."

"Why don't you go and mind your own business," snapped the member. **"This is my third shot!"**

❖

Hawk and Tom were talking in the bar.

Hawk said, "I just got kicked off the course for breaking 60."

Tom looked at him, amazed. "Breaking 60? That's amazing!"

Hawk smiled and said, "Yeah, I never knew a golf buggy could go that fast!"

❖

Doctor wins!

A doctor who golfs has one advantage over the rest of us. **Nobody can read his scorecard**.

A young man and a priest are playing together.

At a short par-3 the priest asks, "What are you going to use on this hole my son?"

The young man says, "An 8-iron, father. How about you?"

The priest says, "I'm going to hit a soft seven and pray."

The young man hits his 8-iron and puts the ball on the green. The priest tops his 7-iron and dribbles the ball out a few yards.

The young man says, "I don't know about you father, but in my church when we pray, **we keep our head down.**"

I once **missed** a hole-in-one – by only 3 strokes.

An elderly couple was in bed one night and the wife asked, "Dear, if I died tomorrow would you get remarried?"

He said "Well, I guess I will, if I feel lonely."

Then she asked "Well, would you two live in this house?"

He replied "Well, I think so."

She asked again, angry now "Well would she sleep in this bed?"

He snickered and said "Yes, this bed is brand new and expensive, there's no reason to get rid of it."

She asked irately, "Well, would she use my golf clubs?"

"No, of course not dear," he replied with a straight, serious face. **"She's left handed."**

T-shirt seen recently at a golf tournament...

"I'm a golf widow... my husband wouldn't quit playing golf, so I shot him."

A Good Score!!!!

Police are called to an apartment and find a woman holding a bloody 5-iron standing over a lifeless man.

The detective asks, "Ma'am, is that your husband?"

"Yes" says the woman.

"Did you hit him with that golf club?"

"Yes, yes, I did." The woman begins to sob, drops the club, and put her hands on her face.

"How many times did you hit him?"

"I don't know, five, six, maybe seven times ... **just put me down for a five."**

Golfer: That can't be my ball, caddie. It looks far too old.

Caddy: It's a long time since we started, sir.

My golf is improving.
Yesterday I hit the ball in one!

Wife to husband: What's your excuse for coming home at this time of the night?
Husband to wife: Golfing with friends, my dear.
Wife to husband: What at 2 AM?
Husband to wife: Yes, we used night clubs.

A gushy reporter told Tiger Woods, "You are spectacular; your name is synonymous with the game of golf. You really know your way around the course. What's your secret?"
Tiger replied, **"The holes are numbered".**

Long ago when men cursed and beat the ground with sticks, it was called witchcraft...
Today, it's called golf.

"I hear you play golf. What is your **handicap**?"
"A wife and three children." Came the reply.

Time to give up Golf

The Golfer got up early, loaded his clubs into the car and proceeded to the Golf course when suddenly there was a torrential downpour with thunder and lightening.

Disappointed he turned and drove back into the house, quietly undressed, and slipped back into bed. There he cuddled up to his wife's back and whispered, "The weather outside is absolutely terrible."

She sleepily replied, **"I know, can you believe my stupid husband went out golfing in that."**

Gary: How come you are so late?
Bill: I had to toss a coin between church and golf.
Gary: Then why are so late?
Bill: I had to toss **18** times.

**The Economy is so bad that...
CEO's are now playing miniature golf.**

Signs & Definitions

Sign erected on the road by The Lions Club of Braxton:

The sign has Lions logo, speed 60 inside the circle, and two graveyard crosses.
The caption reads, "Drive carefully. We have two cemeteries. **No hospital**."

❖

Road sign:

"Don't drink and drive. You'll only spill it."

❖

Sign board behind the car:

"Insured by **Mafias**. You hit me, we hit you."

❖

In a London department store:

"Bargain basement upstairs"

❖

In an office:

"Toilet out of order...... please use floor below."

❖

Sign at the crocodile pond, in the zoo:
"Those who throw objects at the crocodiles will be asked to retrieve them."

Sign on the wall outside the farm:
"No Trespassing. Violators will be shot. Survivors will be shot again."

In a Laundromat:
"Automatic washing machines: please remove all your clothes when the light goes out."

Notice in health food shop window:
"Closed due to illness"

In an office:
"Would the person who took the step ladder yesterday please bring it back or further steps will be taken."

On the door of a repair shop:
>   WE CAN REPAIR **ANYTHING**

(Please knock hard on the door **- the bell doesn't work)**

In a cocktail lounge:
Ladies are requested not to have children in the bar.

Prescription warning:
A prescription of sleeping pills said,
>   "**Warning**: **may cause drowsiness**."

In the office of a doctor:
Specialist in women and other diseases.

On the menu of a restaurant:
Our wines leave you nothing to hope for.

Outside a second-hand shop:
"We exchange **anything** - bicycles, washing machines, etc. Why not bring your wife along and get a wonderful bargain?"

Notice in a farmer's field:
"The farmer allows walkers to cross the field for free, but the bull charges."

In a hotel:
You are invited to take advantage of the chambermaid.

In a laundry:
Ladies, leave your clothes here and spend the afternoon having a good time.

Outside a tailor shop:
Ladies may have a fit upstairs.

In a dry cleaner's:
Drop your trousers here for best results.

Used Cars:
"Why go elsewhere to be cheated? Come here first!"

Spotted in a safari park:
"ELEPHANTS PLEASE STAY IN YOUR CAR"

Advertisement for donkey rides:
Would you like to ride on your own ass?

In a zoo:
Please do not feed the animals. If you have any suitable food, give it to the guard on duty.

In a Hotel in China:
Is forbidden to steal hotel towels please. If you are not a person to do such thing is please not to read notis.

In a hotel:
The flattening of underwear with pleasure is the job of the chambermaid.

Sign in the restaurant:
Dinner Special:
Turkey $2.35; Chicken or Beef $2.25; **Children $2.00**.

Advertisement in Shop:
Guitar for sale.....cheap........no strings attached.

Sign at a barber's saloon:
We need your heads to run our business.

Sign over a Gynaecologist's Office:
"Dr. Jones, at your cervix."

Sign in the laundry shop:
We do not tear your clothing with machinery. We do it **carefully by** hand.

On a Plumber's truck:
   "We repair what your husband fixed."

On an Electrician's truck:
   "Let us remove your shorts."

On a Maternity Room door:
   "Push. Push. Push."

On a Fence:
  "Salesmen welcome! Dog food is expensive!"

At an Optometrist's Office:
   "If you don't see what you're looking for, you've come to the right place."

At a Car Dealership:
"The best way to get back on your feet - miss a car payment."

At the Electric Company:
"We would be **delighted** if you send in your payment. However, if you don't, **you will be**."

In a Restaurant window:
"Don't stand there and be hungry; come on in and get fed up."

In the front yard of a Funeral Home:
"Drive carefully. We'll wait."

In a airline ticket office:
We take your bags and send them in all directions.

CHURCH SIGN:
Going to Heaven?
Get Your Flight Instructions Here

❖

Inside a bowling alley:
"Please be quiet, we need to hear a pin drop."

❖

In the window of an appliance store:
"Don't kill your wife. Let our washing machine do the dirty work."

❖

Life Insurance: A contract that keeps you poor all of your life so that you can **die rich**.

❖

Nurse: A person who wakes you up to give you sleeping pills.

Lunacy of a language

There is no egg in eggplant
No ham in hamburger
And neither pine nor apple in pineapple.
English muffins were not invented in England
French fries were not invented in France.
Quicksand takes you down slowly.
Boxing rings are square.
A guinea pig is neither from Guinea nor is it a pig.
If a vegetarian eats vegetables, what does a humanitarian eat!
And why it is that when I windup my watch It starts…………
But when I wind up this poem, it ends.

School: A place where papa pays and son plays.

At the Bar

A woman and a man are involved in a very bad car accident. Both cars are totally demolished but neither of them is hurt.

The woman says, "Wow, just look at our cars – We're unhurt! It's a miracle. This must be a sign from God that we should be friends."

The man replies, "Oh yes, I agree completely."

The woman says, "And look, here's another miracle. My bottle of wine didn't break. Surely God wants us to drink this wine and celebrate."

She hands the bottle to the man.

The man nods his head in agreement, and drinks half the bottle and hands it back to the woman.

The woman says, **"No, thank you...... I think I'll just wait for the police......."**

Two guys were out drinking when one of them falls off his barstool and falls motionless on the floor.

His buddy tells the bartender, "One thing about Fred, **he knows when to stop"**.

Alcohol is your enemy, but doesn't the bible teach us to **"love your enemies"**.

In a hotel, a phone rings at the reception desk. It is 3.00 am.

"Hello" says a man, "What time does the bar open?"

"Noon, Sir", replies the receptionist.

A few hours later, the phone rings again at the reception desk. It is from the same person.

"What time, did you say, the bar opens?" asked the man

"As I said before, Sir, It opens at noon," replies the receptionist, "if you want to get in, you will have to wait until then, Sir".

"Miss," replies the man, "I don't want to get in.. ....**I want to get out**"

Beer is proof that God loves us and wants us to be happy.

**Sign In A Bar:
'Those Of You Who Are Drinking To Forget,
Please Pay In Advance.'**

❖

**It only takes me ONE drink to get drunk.
The trouble is I can't remember if it's the ninth or tenth.**

❖

A guy asked the bartender for a drink. Then he asked for another. After a few more drinks, the bartender got worried. "What's the matter?" asked the bartender.

"My wife and I got into a fight", explained the guy, "and she vowed not to talk to me for 30 days". He took another drink, and said, "**And tonight is the last night**".

❖

**Alcohol kills slowly.
So what? Who's in a hurry?**

❖

Country Bumpkins / Blondes

A blonde brought a new thermos to work.

Her boss saw it on her desk. "What's that?" he asked.

"Why, that's a special thermos . . . it keeps hot things hot and cold things cold," she replied.

The boss inquires, "What do you have in it?"

The blonde replies, **"Two Popsicles and some coffee."**

Ah Beng ordered a pizza and the waitress asked if she should cut it in six or twelve pieces.

Six, please. I could never eat twelve pieces.

A Moron is buying a TV. "Do you have colour TVs?"

"Sure."

"Give me a green one, please."

One day an employee came in to work with both of his ears bandaged.

When his boss asked him what happened, he explained:

"Yesterday I was ironing a shirt when the phone rang and I accidentally answered the iron instead of the phone!"

"Well," the boss said, "that explains one ear, but what about the other?"

"They called back!"

Police officer: I'm sorry sir, but you will have to come with me.
Driver: Why?
Police officer: You were driving at 120 miles **per hour**!
Driver: But I have only been in my car for **15 minutes!**

Why did 18 Morons go for a movie?
Because below 18 was not allowed.

A moron calls Air India. "How long does it take to fly from Delhi to London?"

"Just a second," says the operator.

"Thank you." says the moron and hangs up.

Did you hear about the idiot who made his chickens drink boiling water?

He thought they would lay **hard boiled eggs**.

A cop saw a blonde down on her knees under a streetlight.

Cop: Can I help you?

Blonde: I dropped my diamond ring and I'm looking for it.

Cop: Did you drop it right here?

Blonde: No, I dropped it about a block away, but the **light is better here**.

Friend: How many women do you believe must a man marry?

Mr. Bean: 16

Friend: Why?

Mr. Bean: Because the priest says 4 richer, 4 poorer, 4 better and 4 worse.

A man stopped his car to ask for directions. "Excuse me, Miss. What's the quickest way to town?"
"Are you walking or driving?" asked the blonde.
"I'm driving."
"Well, that's the quickest way." replied the blonde.

A blonde walks into a store that makes curtains. She says to the clerk, "I would like curtains the size of my computer screen. The clerk says, "Why the size of your computer screen?"

The woman replies, **"Because I've got windows!"**

A moron bought a new mobile phone.

He sent a message to everyone in his Phone Book and said, 'My Mobile No. has changed. **Earlier it was Nokia 3310. Now it is 6610'**

❖

Moron: I am Proud, because my son is in Medical College.
Friend: Really, what is he studying?
Moron: No, he is not studying, **they are studying him.**

❖

Moron: Doctor, in my dreams, I play football every night.
Doctor: Take this tablet, you will be ok.
Moron: Can I take it tomorrow, **tonight is the final game!**

❖

A moron comes back to his car & finds a note saying **'Parking Fine'**

He writes a note and sticks it to a pole **'Thanks for the compliment.'**

❖

A moron was filling up the application form for a job.

He promptly filled columns NAME, AGE, ADDRESS; but got lost on column "SEX".

After much thought, he wrote "THRICE A WEEK".

He was told it was wrong and to write MALE or FEMALE.

Again, moron thought for a long time. Finally, he wrote **"PREFERABLY FEMALES"**.

A moron after the interview:

"Everything went well till the time they asked me to show my testimonials…...

I guess I showed them the **wrong thing....**"

One day two morons were walking down the beach when one said, "Look at that dead bird!"

The other looked up at the sky and said, **"Where???"**

Q: What did the moron do when he missed Bus number 6?
A: He took **Bus number 3 twice**!!!

2 morons were fighting after the exam.
Examiner: Why are you both fighting?
1st moron: This fool left the answer sheet blank.
Examiner: So what?
2nd moron: I did the same thing, now teacher will think that **we both copied**.

Second chance
A moron's wife dies. He is calm, but his wife's lover is crying furiously...
Finally, the moron consoles him: Don't worry buddy, **I will marry again**.

How does a blonde kill a fish?
She drowns it.

Height of miserly
1ˢᵗ Moron: I'm very intelligent. During my honeymoon, I went alone & saved **half** the money.
2ⁿᵈ Moron: I am better than you. During my honeymoon I saved **all** my money. My friend was going & **I sent my wife with him**.

A Blonde went to the Bank to withdraw some money.
"Can you identify yourself?" asked the clerk.
The blonde opened her handbag, took out a mirror, looked into it and said, **"Yes, it is me all right."**

Two blondes are walking down the street.
One notices a compact on the sidewalk and leans down to pick it up. She opens it, looks in the mirror and says, 'Hmm, this person looks **familiar**.'
The second blonde says, 'Here, let me see!'
So the first blonde hands her the compact.
The second one looks in the mirror and says, **'You dummy, it's me!'**

Sick leave

A stressed out worker decided to act crazy to get a few day off from his work by his boss. So he hung himself upside – down on the ceiling and made funny noises.

His co-worker, a blonde, asked him what he was doing. He told her that he was pretending to be a light bulb so that the Boss might think he was 'Crazy' and give him a few days off.

A few minutes later the Boss came into the office and asked, 'What in the name of GOD are you doing?'

The worker replied, "I am a light bulb".

The boss said, 'You are clearly stressed out.' Go home and recuperate for a couple of days.'

The worker jumped down and walked out of the office...

When his co-worker the blonde followed him, the Boss asked her, "....And where do you think you're going?!"

She said, **"I'm going home, too. I can't work in the dark."**

Q. Why can't a blonde dial 911?
A. She can't find the **eleven**.

A blonde was put in a hotel overnight by the Airline due to delay in their flight departure. Next morning, when the steward missed her in the lobby, he called her room and she answered the phone, crying, and said, "I can't get out of the room!"

"Why not?" asked the steward.

She replied, "There are only three doors in here," she sobbed, "one is the bathroom, one is the closet, and one has a sign on it that says **'Do Not Disturb'!"**

Salesman: This computer will cut your workload by 50%.
Office blonde: That's great; I'll take **two** of them.

Moron: People consider me a GOD.
Wife: How do you know?
Moron: When I went to the Park today, everybody said, "**Oh GOD! He has come again."**

All the nations

In Bombay 2 friends met at the bar and were having a chat. "Where is your brother Ali? I haven't seen him for a long time."
"He was in jail; he's just got out."
"Why, what did he do?"
"He was caught bribing a policeman."
"How did he get out?"
"By bribing another."

A Polish immigrant went to the DMV to apply for a driver's license. First, of course, he had to take an eye sight test. The optician showed him a card with the letters:
'C Z W I X N O S T A C Z.'
 "Can you read this?" the optician asked.
 "Read it?" the Polish guy replied, **"I know the guy."**

Pooja: What nationality are you?

Glory: My father is from Iceland and my mother is from Cuba.

Pooja: So you are an **ice cube**?

An American, a Japanese and a Chinese went for a hike one day.

It was very hot. They came upon a small lake and since it was fairly secluded, they took off all their clothes and jumped into the water. Feeling refreshed, the trio decided to pick a few berries while enjoying their "freedom."

As they were crossing an open area, along came a group of ladies from town. Unable to get to their clothes in time, the American and the Japanese covered their privates and the Chinese covered his face while they ran for cover.

After the ladies had left and the men got their clothes back on, the American and the Japanese asked the Chinese why he covered his face rather than his privates.

The Chinese replied, **"I don't know about you, but in my country, it's my face that people would recognize."**

Humour is international

They say if you tell a joke to an Italian, he will laugh once. He will laugh because everyone is laughing.

But if you tell a joke to an Englishman, he will laugh **twice**. Once, because everyone is laughing and again in the middle of the night **when he gets it.**

An Arab student sends an e-mail to his dad, saying:

Dear Dad, Berlin is wonderful, people are nice and I really like it here, but Dad, I am a bit ashamed to arrive at my college with my pure-gold Ferrari 599GTB when all my teachers and many fellow students travel by train.

Your son, Nasser

The next day, Nasser gets a reply to his e-mail from his dad:

My dear loving son, Twenty million US Dollar has just been transferred to your account. Please stop embarrassing us. **Go and get yourself a train too.**

Love, your Dad.

Other Vocations

A man enters a barbershop for a shave. While the barber is foaming him up, he mentions the problems he has getting a close shave around the cheeks.

"I have just the thing," says the barber taking a small wooden ball from a nearby drawer.

"Just place this between your cheek and gum."

The client places the ball in his mouth and the barber proceeds with the closest shave the man has ever experienced.

After a few strokes, the client asks in garbled speech. "And what if I swallow it?"

"No problem," says the barber. "Just bring it back tomorrow **like everyone else does**."

"Your future depends on your dreams"
So go to sleep.

"Hard work never killed anybody"
But why take the risk?

A man takes his place in the theatre, but his seat is too far from the stage.

He whispers to the usher, "This is a mystery, and I have to watch a mystery close up. Get me a better seat, and I'll give you a handsome tip."

The usher moves him into the second row, and the man hands the usher a quarter.

The usher looks at the quarter, leans over and whispers, **"The wife did it."**

A naked girl boarded a taxi. The driver stared.

The girl scolded him, "Never seen a naked girl before?"

The driver replied, "Yes! Seen many before but wondering **where you keep your money to pay taxi fare."**

If at first you don't succeed, skydiving is not for you!

A travelling salesman was held up in the west by a rainstorm and flood. He e-mails his office in NY: "Delayed by storm. Send instructions".

His boss e-mails back**: "Start vacation immediately"**

❖

A diplomat is a person who can convince his wife she looks vulgar in diamonds.

❖

"My big brother has a wonderful job," a boy said to his friend. "He is working with more than 1,000 people under him."

"That sounds like an important job." his friend said, "What does he do?"

"He runs the lawn mower in a cemetery," the first boy said.

❖

Beggar: Sir, give me $2.00 to recharge my mobile and call my girlfriend.
Tourist: Ah, so even a beggar has made a girlfriend!!
Beggar: No Sir, **girlfriend has made me a beggar.**

❖

Boss: We are very keen on cleanliness. Did you wipe your feet on the mat as you came in?
New employee: Yes, sir.
Boss: We are also keen on truthfulness. There is **no mat**.

❖

The businessman dragged himself home and dropped exhausted to his chair. His wife brought him a tall cool drink and said, "My, you look tired. You must have had a hard day today. What happened to make you so exhausted?"
"It was terrible," her husband said**. "The computer broke down and all of us had to do our own thinking."**

❖

Computer related

Caller: Hello, is this Tech Support?

Tech: Yes, it is. How may I help you?

Caller: The cup holder in front of my PC is broken and I am within my warranty period. How do I go about getting that fixed?

Tech: How did you get this cup holder? Did you receive as part of a promotional, at a trade show? Has it got any trade mark on it?

Caller: It came with my computer; I don't know anything about a promotional. **It just has '52X' printed on it.**

A Dell technician advised his customer to put his troubled floppy back in the drive and close the door.

The customer asked the tech to hold on, and was heard putting the phone down, getting up and crossing the room **to close the door to his room**.

Another Compaq technician received a call from a man complaining that the system wouldn't read word processing files from his old diskettes.

After trouble-shooting for magnets and heat failed to diagnose the problem, it was found that the customer had labelled the diskettes, and then rolled them into the **typewriter to type the labels**.

Another AST customer was asked to send a copy of her defective diskettes. A few days later a letter arrived from the customer along with **photocopies of the floppies**.

A Dell technician received a call from a customer who was enraged because his computer had told him he was "bad and an invalid".

The tech explained that the computer's "bad command" and "invalid" responses **shouldn't be taken personally.**

A confused caller to IBM was having troubles printing documents. He told the technician that the computer had said it "couldn't find printer". The user had also tried turning the computer screen to face the printer - but that his computer **still couldn't "see" the printer**.

Another customer called Compaq tech support to say her brand-new computer wouldn't work. She said she unpacked the unit, plugged it in and sat there for 20 minutes waiting for something to happen.
When asked what happened when she pressed the power switch, she asked **"What power switch?"**

AST technical support had a caller complaining that her mouse was hard to control with the dust cover on.
The cover turned out to be the plastic bag the mouse was packaged in.

Little boy's prayer:

Dear God, please send clothes for all those poor ladies on dad's computer - Amen

A woman called the Canon help desk with a problem with her printer.
The tech asked her if she was running it "under Windows."
The woman responded, "No, my desk is next to the door. But that is a good point. The man sitting in the cubicle next to me is **under a window and his printer is working fine.**"

**On the door of a computer store:
"Out for a quick byte."**

Did you hear about the baby born in the **high-tech** delivery room? **It was cordless!**

Miscellaneous

The doorbell rang and the lady of the house discovered a workman, complete with tool chest, on the front porch.

"Madam," he announced, "I'm the piano tuner."

The lady exclaimed, "Why, I didn't send for a piano tuner."

The man replied, **"I know you didn't, but your neighbours did."**

A real estate salesman had just closed his first deal, only to discover that the piece of land he had sold was completely under water.

"That customer's going to come back here pretty mad," he said to his boss. "Should I give him his money back?"

"Money back? Are you crazy???" roared the boss. "What kind of salesman are you? **Get out there and sell him a houseboat."**

The sheriff of a small town was also the town's veterinarian. One night the phone rang, and his wife answered.

An agitated voice inquired, "Is your husband there?"

"Do you require his services as a sheriff or as a vet?" the wife asked.

"**Both!**" was the reply. "We can't get our dog's mouth open, and there's a burglar in it."

Love thy neighbour. But don't get caught.

I met a friend the other day.
"Hi," I said, "I haven't seen you for a long time. What are you doing nowadays?"
"Oh," said the guy, "I am selling furniture."
"Ah! Things are going well then."
"Not so well," he replied, **"It's my furniture."**

Saddam Hussein has now agreed to weapons inspections. The bad news is that he wants **Arthur Andersen to do it.**

Mr. Johnson walked anxiously to the house and knocked. When a nice old lady answered, he sadly said, "I'm sorry, madam, but I have some bad news. I'm afraid I have run over your cat. I… I would like to replace it."

The little lady looked him up and down and said, **"I'm game, but how are you at catching mice?"**

A man at the airline counter tells the rep. "I'd like this bag to go to Berlin, this one to California, and this one to London."

The rep says, "I'm sorry sir. We can't do that."

The man replied: **"Nonsense. That is what you did last time I flew with you."**

After hearing that one of the patients in a mental hospital had saved another from a suicide attempt by pulling him out of a bathtub, the director reviewed the rescuer's file and called him into his office.

"Mr. James, your records and your heroic behaviour indicate that you're ready to go home. I'm only sorry that the man you saved later killed himself with a rope around the neck."

"Oh, he didn't kill himself," Mr. James replied. **"I hung him up to dry."**

Two cab drivers met. "Hey," asked one, "what's the idea of painting one side of your cab red and the other side blue?"

"Well," the other responded, "when I get into an accident, you should see how all the witnesses **contradict each other**."

God made relatives; Thank God we **can choose our friends.**

One friend to another, "My new horse is very well-mannered."

"Really?"

"Yes, every time we come to a jump **he stops and lets me go first!**"

❖

Director: In the last scene of this film, you have to jump from the 13th floor.

Actor: But in case I die?

Director: It does not matter; it is the last scene in the film.

❖

Man tells his MP: My son's a drug addict, my daughter's a prostitute, my wife's a gambler.

MP: Isn't there anything positive in your family?

Man: Yes, I am **HIV positive**.

❖

A radical feminist is getting on a bus when, just in front of her, a man gets up from his seat.

The chauvinistic woman pushes him back onto the seat.

A few minutes later, the man tries to get up again. She is still insulted so she refuses to let him up again.

Finally, the man says, **"Look, lady, you've got to let me get up. I'm twelve blocks past my stop already."**

A police officer in a small town stopped a motorist who was speeding down Main Street.

The motorist tried to explain his innocence.

"Just be quiet. You are going to jail until the chief gets back." snapped the officer

A few hours later the officer looked at his prisoner and said, "Lucky for you that the chief is at his daughter's wedding. He'll be in a good mood when he gets back."

"Don't count on it," answered the guy in the cell. **"I'm the groom".**

A guy was driving when a policeman pulled him over. He rolled down his window and said to the officer, "Is there a problem, Officer?"

"No problem at all. I just observed your safe driving and am pleased to award you a $5,000 Safe Driver Award. Congratulations. What do you think you're going to do with the money?"

He thought for a minute and said, "Well, I guess I'll go get that drivers' license."

The lady sitting in the passenger seat said to the policeman, "Oh, don't pay attention to him - he's a smart ass when he's drunk and stoned."

The guy from the back seat said, "I TOLD you guys we wouldn't get far in a stolen car!"

At that moment, there was a knock from the trunk and a muffled voice said, **"Are we over the border yet?"**

A lady greeted her guest at the front door and invited her in. The guest looked a bit frightened as the old family dog stood there staring at her.

"Don't worry about that old dog," the lady of the house said. "He's just like one of the family".

"Which one?" the guest asked.

A man went to the chemist to buy 6 tablets of Viagra, cut in **quarters**. The Chemist said that quarters would not work in full.

The Man said, "I know. I am 70 and sex is out of the question. I just want to take enough so that **I don't wet my shoes when I ease myself**."

Say it with flowers

A gentleman entered a busy florist shop that displayed a large sign that read **"Say It with Flowers."**

"Wrap up one rose" he told the florist.

"Only one?" the florist asked.

"Just one," the customer replied **"I'm a man of few words."**

Two Norwegians are drinking in a bar.

Ole says, "Did you know that lions have sex 5 to 10 times a week?"

"Oh no," says Svenson, "Why didn't you tell me earlier. **I just joined Rotary**."

In a circus stunt, a lady and a lion were kissing each other inside a cage.

The Ring master proudly challenged the audience, "Can anyone do it?"

One person from the audience slowly answered, **"I can, but first take the stupid lion out"**

❖

During a visit to the mental asylum, a visitor asked the Director what the criterion was which defined whether or not a patient should be institutionalized.

"Well," said the Director, "we fill up a bathtub, and then we offer a teaspoon, a teacup and a bucket to the patient and ask him or her to empty the bathtub."

"Oh, I understand," said the visitor. "A normal person would use the bucket because it's bigger than the spoon or the teacup.

"No." said the Director, "A normal person would pull the plug. **Do you want a bed near the window?"**

Thought Provoking Questions!

If you take an **Oriental** person and spin him around several times, does he become **disoriented**?

If people from Poland are called **"Poles"**, why aren't people from Holland called **"Holes"**?

Do infants enjoy **infancy** as much as adults enjoy **adultery**?

If Fed Ex and UPS were to merge, would they call it **Fed UP**?

Do Lipton Tea employees take **coffee** breaks?

If it's true that we are here to help others, then what exactly are the others here **for?**

If olive oil comes from olives, where does **baby** oil come from?

Why is it called a building when it is already **built**?

Isn't it a bit unnerving that doctors call what they do "**practice**"?

In a psychology class, after the teacher and students had discussed on the subject of "feelings", the teacher asked the students, "How would you best describe the difference between **stress, tension and panic**?"

A student in the back row stood up and said, "Sir, **Stress** is when wife is pregnant, **Tension** is when the girlfriend is pregnant, and **Panic** is when **both are pregnant**."

Wise observation:
The world is like a fruitcake. It wouldn't be complete without a few nuts.

Gallagher opened the morning newspaper and was dumbfounded to read in the obituary column that he had died. He quickly phoned his best friend, Finney.

"Did you see the paper?" asked Gallagher. "They say I died!!"

"Yes, I saw it!" replied Finney. **"Where are you calling from?"**